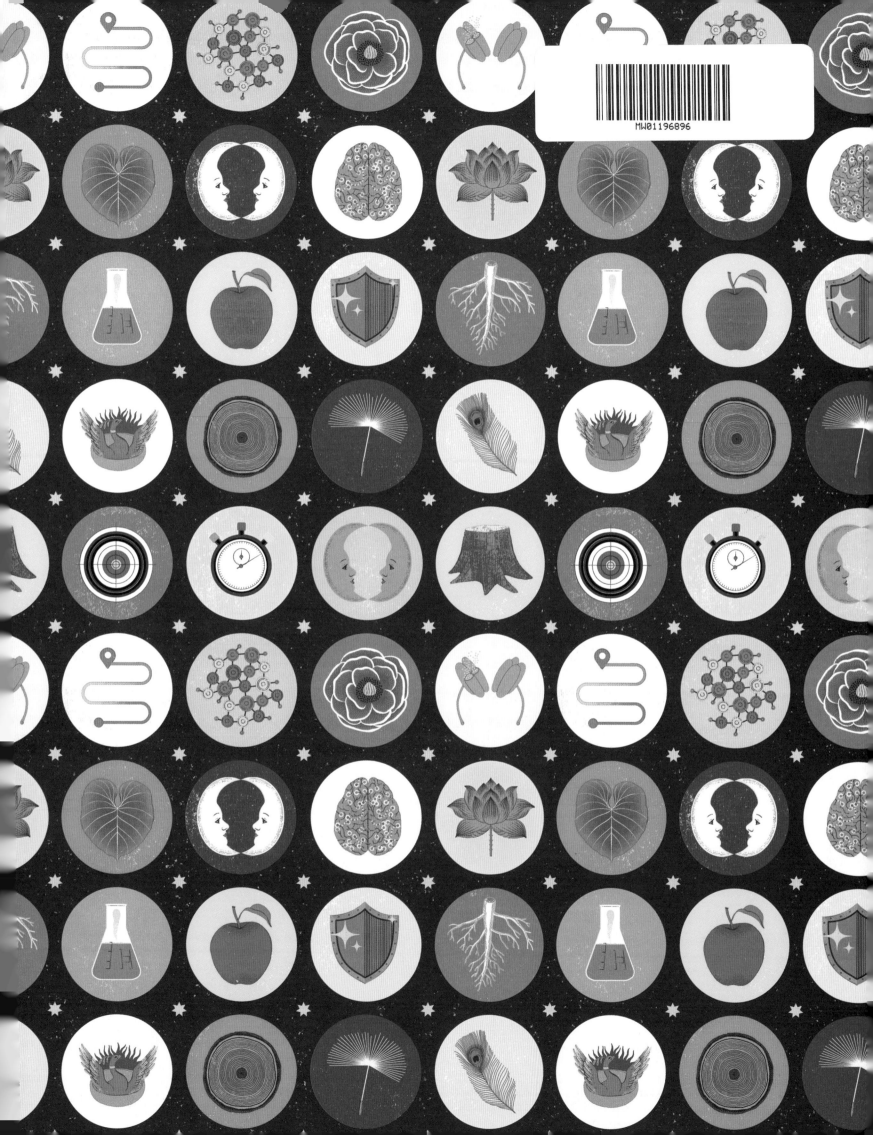

SUPER POWERED PLANTS

By **Soledad Romero Mariño**

Illustrated by **Sonia Pulido**

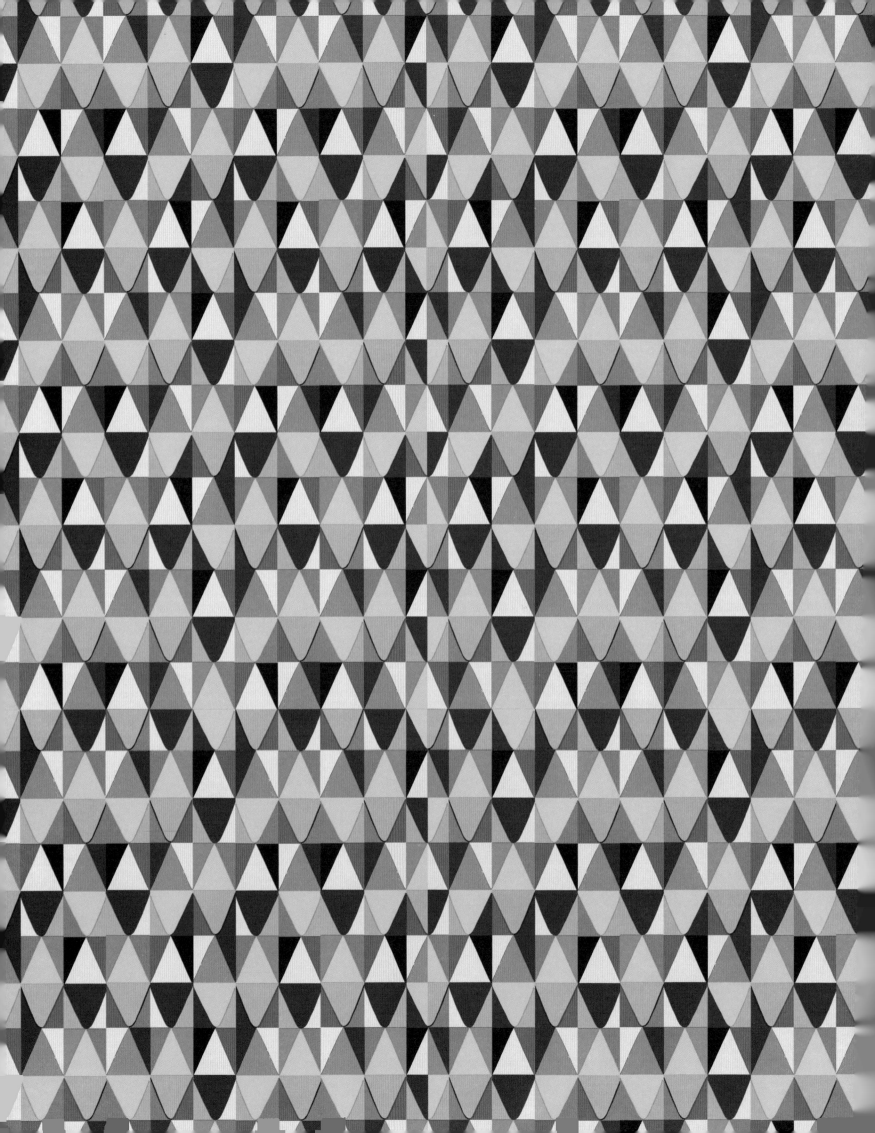

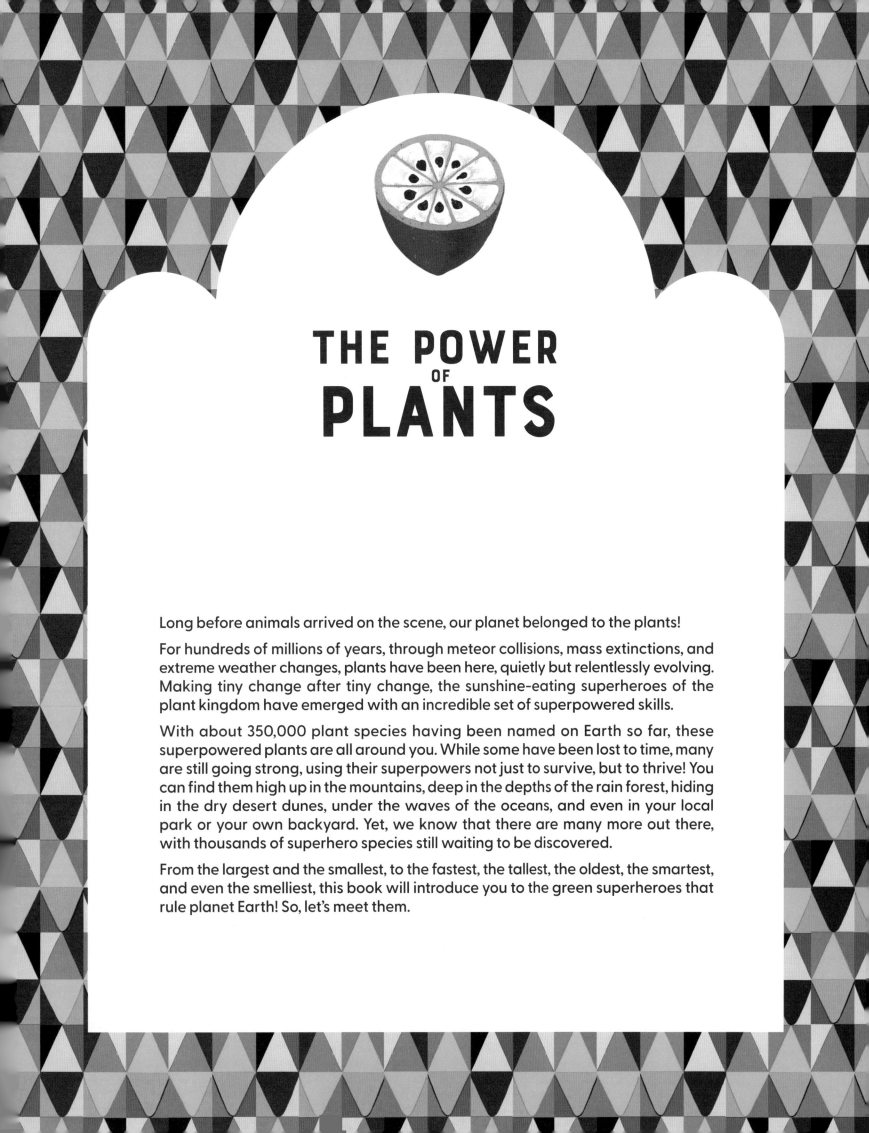

THE POWER
OF
PLANTS

Long before animals arrived on the scene, our planet belonged to the plants!

For hundreds of millions of years, through meteor collisions, mass extinctions, and extreme weather changes, plants have been here, quietly but relentlessly evolving. Making tiny change after tiny change, the sunshine-eating superheroes of the plant kingdom have emerged with an incredible set of superpowered skills.

With about 350,000 plant species having been named on Earth so far, these superpowered plants are all around you. While some have been lost to time, many are still going strong, using their superpowers not just to survive, but to thrive! You can find them high up in the mountains, deep in the depths of the rain forest, hiding in the dry desert dunes, under the waves of the oceans, and even in your local park or your own backyard. Yet, we know that there are many more out there, with thousands of superhero species still waiting to be discovered.

From the largest and the smallest, to the fastest, the tallest, the oldest, the smartest, and even the smelliest, this book will introduce you to the green superheroes that rule planet Earth! So, let's meet them.

TABLE OF
CONTENTS

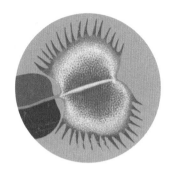

16

PRICKLY PEAR
The relentless thorny invader

18

NEPTUNE GRASS
The eco-warrior of the seas

20

SACRED LOTUS
The dazzling jewel
rising from the mud

22

SUNFLOWER
The flower that follows the sun

32

SKELETON FLOWER
The mysterious magician

34

STRANGLER FIG
The boa constrictor tree

36

SPOTTED SPIDER ORCHID
The tarantula trickster

38

DANDELION
The seeds that take to the skies

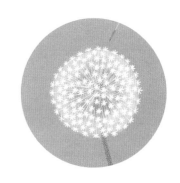

48

WHISTLING THORN
The musical tree of the savanna

50

QUAKING ASPEN
The trembling giant of giants

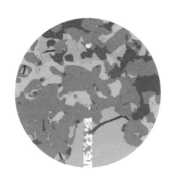

52

WELWITSCHIA
The living fossil

54

ROOTLESS DUCKWEED
The small but mighty multiplier

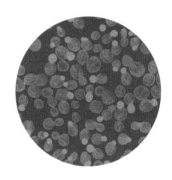

THE SUPERPOWERS

Whether they're growing up tall toward the sunlight, spreading their seeds far and wide, fighting off attackers, or attracting the perfect pollinators, plants have developed superpowers to meet their every need. They have it all covered, from marvelous mimicry and powerful poisons to superspeeds and mind-blowing resilience. Let's take a look at the superpowers of the plant kingdom.

SUPER
MOBILITY

Certain plants are natural explorers. While some climb, some float, and others send their seeds flying through the air, these superpowered plants can really cover some ground.

DANDELION
PASSION FRUIT
QUAKING ASPEN
ROOTLESS DUCKWEED
STRANGLER FIG
SUNFLOWER

SUPER
SPEED

While most plants may not look like fast movers, some species are surprisingly speedy, shooting up toward the sky, snapping their leaves shut in a flash, or spreading over vast areas astonishingly quickly.

PASSION FRUIT
ROOTLESS DUCKWEED
SANDBOX
SENSITIVE PLANT
SUNFLOWER
TITAN ARUM
VENUS FLYTRAP

SUPER
ROOTS

Superpowered root systems can work wonders, from finding water in the dry sand of the desert to anchoring plants to the seabed or even enabling them to grow high up in the forest canopy.

AFRICAN BAOBAB
JACKAL FOOD
NEPTUNE GRASS
QUAKING ASPEN
SPOTTED SPIDER ORCHID
WELWITSCHIA

SUPER
TEAMWORK

Instead of going it alone, many plant species benefit from the amazing power of teamwork. Forming relationships with other plants, and sometimes with animals, these collaborations can have huge benefits for the plants involved.

NEPTUNE GRASS
QUAKING ASPEN
ROOTLESS DUCKWEED
STRANGLER FIG
WELWITSCHIA
WHISTLING THORN

SUPER
TRUNK

Some tree trunks are capable of extraordinary feats, growing to enormous sizes, storing immense amounts of water, or protecting themselves from forest fires and unwelcome visitors.

AFRICAN BAOBAB
COAST REDWOOD
SWEET CHESTNUT

SUPER
MIMICRY

Some plants are true tricksters. Often with the aim of attracting pollinators, many have learned to imitate the shapes and even the smells of the world around them.

SPOTTED SPIDER ORCHID
TITAN ARUM

SUPER
REGENERATION

From repopulating forests after wildfires to generating clones, the power of renewal lets some plants come back fighting after every challenge!

COAST REDWOOD
PRICKLY PEAR
QUAKING ASPEN

SUPER
SENSITIVITY

Certain plants are hypersensitive to touch. This intriguing superpower is sometimes used in self-defense and sometimes as part of a deadly attack.

SENSITIVE PLANT
VENUS FLYTRAP

SUPER
SEED

Holding the promise of new life, a plant's seed is its greatest treasure. Plants are on a mission to spread them far and wide, and they have many ingenious ways of doing so.

COAST REDWOOD
DANDELION
PASSION FRUIT
SACRED LOTUS
SUNFLOWER

SUPER
PROTECTION

From spikes, thorns, and deadly poisons to armies of aggressive ants, many plants have perfected the art of self-defense.

PRICKLY PEAR
SANDBOX
SWEET CHESTNUT
WHISTLING THORN

SUPER
LONGEVITY

Some plant species have adapted to suit their environment so perfectly that they can live for what seems like forever.

AFRICAN BAOBAB
COAST REDWOOD
NEPTUNE GRASS
QUAKING ASPEN
SWEET CHESTNUT
TITAN ARUM
WELWITSCHIA

SUPER
SUBSTANCES

Plants use clever chemical substances for all kinds of reasons: to lure in pollinators, to ward off enemies, or even to communicate with other plants.

JACKAL FOOD
OLEANDER
STRANGLER FIG
VENUS FLYTRAP
WHISTLING THORN

SUPER
FRUIT

Some fruits are delicious, some are spiky, some float on water, and some even explode, but they all have the same aim of protecting and dispersing the priceless seeds inside.

AFRICAN BAOBAB
NEPTUNE GRASS
PASSION FRUIT
PRICKLY PEAR
SANDBOX
SWEET CHESTNUT

SUPER
RESILIENCE

Whether it's soaring temperatures or water scarcity and droughts, some of these supertough plants can cope with a lot, ensuring their survival in even the most extreme conditions.

AFRICAN BAOBAB
COAST REDWOOD
JACKAL FOOD
OLEANDER
PRICKLY PEAR
SACRED LOTUS
SANDBOX TREE
SENSITIVE PLANT
SKELETON FLOWER
WELWITSCHIA
WHISTLING THORN

SUPER
FLOWER

Bright, bold, and beautiful, a plant's flowers often play a starring role in pollination, using their color, size, and fragrance to lure in insects from far and wide.

AFRICAN BAOBAB
DANDELION
JACKAL FOOD
OLEANDER
PASSION FRUIT
SACRED LOTUS
SKELETON FLOWER
SPOTTED SPIDER ORCHID
STRANGLER FIG
SUNFLOWER
SWEET CHESTNUT
TITAN ARUM

SUPER
INTELLIGENCE

Certain plants are supersmart. From regulating the temperature of their flowers to stealing food and water from other plants, many have developed clever strategies to guarantee their survival.

JACKAL FOOD
NEPTUNE GRASS
OLEANDER
ROOTLESS DUCKWEED
SACRED LOTUS
SENSITIVE PLANT
STRANGLER FIG
VENUS FLYTRAP
WELWITSCHIA

SUPER
LEAF

Some catch tasty insects to munch on as a snack and others grow to extraordinary sizes, but a plant's leaves are all capable of the most magnificent superpower of all—using photosynthesis to turn sunlight into food.

DANDELION
NEPTUNE GRASS
SACRED LOTUS
VENUS FLYTRAP
WELWITSCHIA

Throughout this book, each plant had been awarded a star rating that reflects the number of superpowers it has.

SCIENTIFIC NAME:

DIONAEA MUSCIPULA

CLASS: Magnoliopsida
ORDER: Caryophyllales
FAMILY: Droseraceae

VENUS FLYTRAP

The fearsome, flesh-eating beauty

This pretty, but deadly, plant uses its good looks to lure and trap unsuspecting prey. And it's not just flies on the menu—spiders, beetles, and even small frogs are all at risk of becoming lunch for this snappy predator.

THIS PLANT IS NOT ACTIVE DURING WINTER. IT RESTS AND BUILDS UP STRENGTH FOR SPRING.

SUPER LEAF

These colorful, sweet-smelling leaves are purposely designed to attract insects and small animals. But all is not as it seems—as soon as an unsuspecting creature touches the surface of the plant, the jawlike leaves snap shut around them. The victim is digested over the following week, before the plant opens up its leaves once again, ready for its next meal.

SUPER SENSITIVITY

Tiny hairs, called trichomes, on the plant's leaves detect even the lightest touch from prey. When triggered, they release an electric charge that causes the trap to close at lightning speed. Sometimes, if a creature won't provide enough nutritional value to make digestion worthwhile, the leaves will open up, allowing the lucky creature to make an escape.

SUPER SUBSTANCES

The leaves contain a red pigment, called anthocyanin, which lures small insects toward the trap. Once an insect is shut inside, the plant secretes a shiny, sticky substance called mucilage. This acts like glue, sealing the edge of the trap and keeping wriggling prey locked inside. The plant then releases digestive enzymes that break down and absorb the nutrients from the creature. Yum!

SUPER INTELLIGENCE

This plant still uses photosynthesis to get most of its energy from sunlight, but the extra snacks that it traps and digests provide additional nutrients and proteins that it can't get from the poor-quality soil where it grows. This smart strategy means it is able to thrive in places where other plants would struggle.

SUPER SPEED

Even the quickest of critters don't stand a chance against this superspeedy plant. Once triggered, the trap can shut in less than half a second!

Venus flytraps cope well with fire. They rely on forest fires happening from time to time to minimize competition from other plants.

SIZE
Leaf stalks can grow to about 4 inches tall and flower stalks can grow to 12 inches tall. The traps themselves measure about 1¼ inches across.

COLOR
The leaves are green on the outside and a rich red or orange on the inside. Its flowers are white.

SPECIAL FEATURES
The sensitive trigger hairs on the leaves have to be touched at least twice within 30 seconds to activate the trap, meaning the plant doesn't waste energy on false alarms.

LIFESPAN
20 to 30 years in ideal conditions.

HABITAT
Native to the marshes and wetlands of the southeastern United States, the plant also grows in other places with similar conditions.

REPRODUCTION
Reproduces by seeds, producing tiny black seeds that are only ⁵⁄₁₂₈ inch across.

ENEMIES
Urban growth and habitat loss have reduced the wild population and Venus flytraps are now an endangered species.

AFRICAN BAOBAB

The upside-down tree of legends

SCIENTIFIC NAME:
ADANSONIA DIGITATA

CLASS: Magnoliopsida
ORDER: Malvales
FAMILY: Malvaceae

The sacred baobab tree, with its towering trunk and its spindly branches, is a symbol of Africa. Celebrated since ancient times, these gentle giants provide water, food, and shelter to the people and animals of the savanna.

IT'S IMPOSSIBLE TO KNOW THE AGE OF A BAOBAB BY COUNTING ITS RINGS, BECAUSE THEY FADE AS THE TREE GROWS.

SUPER RESILIENCE

The thick bark of the baobab's trunk is remarkably strong. It can withstand the soaring temperatures of wildfires and will even grow back if damaged. The tree's seeds are just as tough, being able to germinate more than five years after they originally form.

SUPER LONGEVITY

These African giants can live for more than 1,000 years, with one of the oldest-known trees reaching an extraordinary 2,450 years old. It generally takes up to 200 years for the tree to reach maturity and begin producing fruit.

SUPER FLOWER

Unusually, the huge, white blossoms of the baobab bloom overnight. They open up their petals as the sun sets, with their sweet-smelling nectar luring in bats and other nocturnal pollinators. But the bats need to be quick, because the flowers only last for 24 hours!

SUPER ROOTS

The baobab's roots spread out far and wide in search of water in the dry soil of the savanna. The roots can extend a whopping 165 feet from the tree, but they stay close to the surface, because this is where the most moisture can be found.

SUPER FRUIT

While the baobab's fruit might not look tasty on first glance—some people say it looks like a dead rat hanging from the tree's branches—it's actually delicious! It's also healthy and packed full of vitamin C.

SUPER TRUNK

The tree's barrel-like trunk contains huge stores of water that are essential for its survival. This iconic storage tank of a trunk can hold a superimpressive 26,400 gallons of water, making up a huge 76 percent of the tree itself.

During the dry season, elephants use their tusks to rip open baobab trunks, finding water and quenching their thirst.

SIZE
Up to 80 feet tall. The trunk can grow to 30 feet across.

COLOR
Black, red, or gray bark and white flowers.

SPECIAL FEATURES
With its huge trunk and thin branches that look like a root system, the baobab tree is often known as the "upside-down tree."

LIFESPAN
Typically between 800 and 1,000 years, with some reaching more than 2,000 years.

HABITAT
Native to tropical Africa, as well as small areas of southern Arabia and several Atlantic Ocean and Indian Ocean islands around the African continent. Madagascar is well known for its baobabs, with six different species calling the island home.

REPRODUCTION
Reproduces by seeds. The first flowers appear when the tree is 20 years old.

ENEMIES
Climate change is threatening baobab trees, because they struggle with rising temperatures.

PRICKLY PEAR

THIS FEISTY PLANT IS PROUDLY DEPICTED ON THE COAT OF ARMS OF MEXICO, ITS NATIVE HOME.

The relentless thorny invader

Like a fierce queen ruling over the desert, this unstoppable plant wears a crown of red, orange, and yellow flowers. A shield of spines offers protection as the warrior plant forges forward, continually colonizing new lands across the desert.

SCIENTIFIC NAME:

OPUNTIA FICUS-INDICA

CLASS: Magnoliopsida
ORDER: Caryiphyllales
FAMILY: Cactaceae

SUPER
PROTECTION

This plant wears an armor of shockingly sharp, prickly spikes. Hungry creatures better beware, because clusters of long, hard barbs shield the plant's flat, oval-shape stems (called pads) and smaller hairlike prickles protect its precious fruit.

SUPER
REGENERATION

The prickly pear uses a clever tactic to spread at an astonishing rate—any pad that falls from the plant can take root in the ground and grow into a new shrub wherever it lands.

SUPER
RESILIENCE

This tough plant is completely equipped for the extremes. It stores water in its pads, enabling it to survive in the dry desert, under the scorching heat of the sun, but it can also withstand freezing cold temperatures and strong winds.

SUPER
FRUIT

The round fruit of the prickly pear is a fleshy berry filled with seeds—delicious, if you can get past the savage spikes! The spines are superthin and strong when the fruit is still green, but they turn fragile (and get easier to remove) as it ripens. Remember to wear gloves when handling the fruit and always peel before eating!

The extensive root system of the prickly pear preserves the soil by protecting it against erosion from wind and water.

SIZE
Up to 25 feet tall and 13¾ inches across.

COLOR
Green pads and red, orange, and yellow flowers. The fruit starts off green but changes to yellow and red as it ripens.

SPECIAL FEATURES
The prickly pear doesn't have leaves. Instead, it has pads that can branch out from the trunk.

LIFESPAN
Up to 100 years.

HABITAT
Native to Mexico, but always expanding its range. The plant now grows in dry, arid regions throughout the world.

REPRODUCTION
Reproduces by seeds and also by cloning itself from fallen pads.

ENEMIES
Cochineal insects can attack the prickly pear, living underneath its protective spikes and taking food and water from the plant.

NEPTUNE GRASS

The eco-warrior of the seas

SCIENTIFIC NAME:
POSIDONIA OCEANICA

CLASS: Liliopsida
ORDER: Alismatales
FAMILY: Posidoniaceae

OFTEN MISTAKEN FOR SEAWEED, NEPTUNE GRASS IS ACTUALLY AN AQUATIC PLANT WITH ROOTS, STALKS, LEAVES, FLOWERS, AND FRUIT.

Sprawling underwater meadows of Neptune grass carpet the seabed of the Mediterranean. These beautiful plants are fighting climate change in their own quiet, but incredibly powerful, way—absorbing more carbon dioxide than the equivalent area of the Amazon rain forest.

SUPER TEAMWORK

This clever plant is made up of several different parts, all working together as one. It grows in "tufts," each made up of a mat of rhizomes (a type of special stem) with roots at one end and a group of four to eight leaves at the other.

SUPER LONGEVITY

Each tuft of Neptune grass can live for many years, because the leaves are constantly replaced. The meadows are some of the longest-living organisms on our planet, with one meadow off the coast of Spain reaching a staggering 100,000 years old.

SUPER FRUIT

Seagrasses are the only plants on Earth to flower and produce fruit under the ocean's waves. Often known as a sea olive, the nutlike fruit floats around in the currents until the flesh rots away and the single seed drops down to the seabed, ready to grow.

SUPER ROOTS

The strong roots of Neptune grass are perfectly adapted to keep the plant safely fixed to the seabed, allowing for it to colonize areas that would be off-limits to rootless marine organisms, such as algae.

SUPER INTELLIGENCE

This smart plant has a clever tactic to maximize its energy production. It positions its oldest leaves, which are the most active for photosynthesis, on the outside of the tuft and keeps the younger, less productive leaves on the inside.

SUPER LEAF

The superpowered leaves of Neptune grass are vital for the survival of the planet. These environmentally friendly plants generate so much oxygen that they have been called "the lungs of the sea." They are heroes in our battle against climate change.

Neptune grass provides the perfect home for fish, crabs, sea urchins and even turtles. Many animals use the meadows as a nursery or hiding place.

SIZE
Meadows can stretch for several miles. The leaves can grow up to 3 feet 3 inches in length and the roots can grow up to 6 inches.

COLOR
Green leaves and yellowish green flowers.

SPECIAL FEATURES
Along with the roots, the plant's rhizomes stretch into the sand, growing both horizontally and vertically, anchoring the grass to the seabed.

LIFESPAN
A meadow can live for many thousands of years.

HABITAT
Found only in the Mediterranean Sea.

REPRODUCTION
Neptune grass extends its range by producing "runners" (new plant shoots) at the bottom of the stalk. It also colonizes new areas using seeds.

ENEMIES
Human activities, including fishing, coastal development, pollution, and rising sea temperatures caused by climate change, all threaten the survival of Neptune grass.

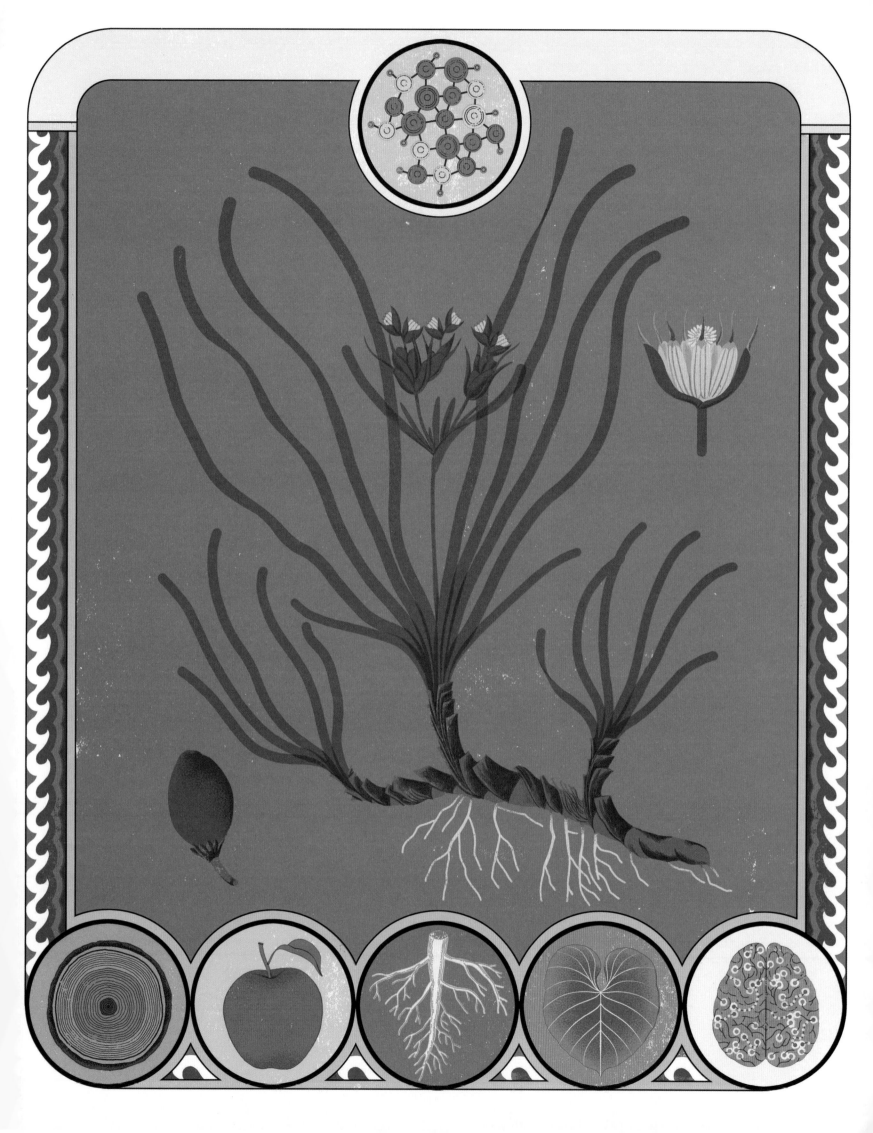

SCIENTIFIC
NAME:
**NELUMBO
NUCIFERA**

CLASS: Magnoliopsida
ORDER: Proteales
FAMILY: Nelumbonaceae

SACRED LOTUS

The dazzling jewel rising from the mud

This aquatic plant is a symbol of purity, with its stunning, bright flowers emerging from the murky depths of the marshland, ready to bask in the sunlight above.

LINKED TO THE SUN IN HINDUISM, AND PURITY IN BUDDHISM, THE LOTUS FLOWER IS SPIRITUALLY SIGNIFICANT TO MANY DIFFERENT COMMUNITIES IN ASIA.

SUPER
SEED

When the seeds of the sacred lotus plant are released into the water, many are eaten by animals; others sprout immediately and begin to grow, but the remainder do something amazingly special. They wait, hiding silently in the muddy sediment, biding their time until the conditions are just right. This waiting game can last years, centuries, or even longer—one seed is known to have germinated after an amazing 1,300 years!

The root system of the sacred lotus has an incredible ability to absorb pollutants, enabling it to cleanse and improve the water quality of its ecosystem.

SUPER
INTELLIGENCE

Almost unbelievably, this plant can regulate the temperature of its flowers. Even if the surroundings fall to a chilly 50°F or rise to a scorching 115°F, the flower will stay at a comfortable 86–96.8°F. This smart strategy attracts insects, providing a warm place for pollination, and also encourages the flowers to develop.

SUPER
FLOWER

The flower of the sacred lotus is the national flower of both India and Vietnam, and it's no wonder that it's popular, with its striking beauty and sweet fragrance. But make sure to enjoy them while you can, because the blooms typically only last for a few days.

SIZE
Up to 6 feet 6 inches tall. The flowers can grow to 1 foot across and the leaves can grow up to 3 feet 3 inches across.

COLOR
Green stalk and leaves. In the wild, the flower is typically white, but it can also be white and pink.

SUPER
RESILIENCE

This delicate-looking plant is surprisingly tough. Growing in the muddy waters of shallow lakes and ponds, river deltas, and marshland, it thrives in waterlogged conditions where other plants would struggle.

SPECIAL FEATURES
The stalks that join the stem of the plant to the leaves can grow to a lengthy 8 feet 3 inches and are covered with prickles.

LIFESPAN
The flower lives only for a few days, but the seeds can survive for centuries.

SUPER
LEAF

The huge, round leaves of the sacred lotus keep the plant happy and healthy in its muddy home. The leaves are covered in tiny bumps, called papillae, which themselves are covered with tough, waxy tubes. This special surface gives the plant the unique ability to repel water. As the water rolls off the leaves, it collects dirt, keeping the surface clean and dry.

HABITAT
Native to Southeast Asia, but now widespread and found on other continents where it has been introduced in gardens.

REPRODUCTION
The plant releases hundreds of thousands of seeds every year. It also reproduces by spreading rhizomes (a type of special stem) into the muddy ground.

SUNFLOWER

The flower that follows the sun

Bright yellow and endlessly cheerful, the sunflower plant stands tall and proud in gardens around the world, using its sunny superpower to grow with gusto.

SCIENTIFIC NAME:

HELIANTHUS ANNUUS

CLASS: Magnoliopsida
ORDER: Asterales
FAMILY: Asteraceae

ONLY YOUNG SUNFLOWERS TRACK THE SUN. ONCE MATURE, THE FLOWER HEADS ALWAYS FACE EAST.

SUPER
FLOWER

The well-loved "flower" of this beautiful plant is actually a flower head (or an inflorescence) that is made up of a lot of smaller flowers. The large yellow-brown area in the middle contains a huge number of tiny flowers, called disk florets. These are surrounded by one or two rows of ray florets, which look like bright yellow petals but are actually individual flowers themselves. Each flower head is a flower extravaganza!

With so many flowers packed tightly together in one place, it's not surprising that sunflower heads are incredibly popular with pollinators, especially bees.

SUPER
SPEED

Ready, steady, grow! With plenty of food, water, and sunshine, this cheerful plant can grow at an impressive speed. Some varieties reach a mighty 13 feet in only three months.

SIZE
Up to 13 feet tall for some varieties. The flower heads can reach a remarkable 1 foot across.

COLOR
Green stem and yellow or brown flower heads.

SUPER
MOBILITY

Did you think that plants cannot move? Well, think again, because the sunflower is able to do just that. Sunflower buds are heliotropic, which means that their flower heads can track the movement of the sun, facing east at sunrise and gradually turning west as the day goes on and the sun begins to set. Incredibly, it resets its east-facing position at night, ready for the morning.

SPECIAL FEATURES
The leaves of the plant are long, with serrated edges, the roots are capable of delving deep into the soil, and the stem is thick, upright, and solid.

LIFESPAN
One year.

HABITAT
Native to North and Central America, it grows in both dry and moist soil. The plant can be traced back to Mexico to about 2600 BCE, but it has now spread around the world.

SUPER
SEED

Despite the name, sunflower seeds are technically the fruit of the plant, and each flower head can produce hundreds or even thousands of them. The beautifully arranged seeds form an almost perfect spiral, enabling the maximum number of seeds possible to be packed into the sunflower head without any overlapping.

REPRODUCTION
Reproduces by spreading its dark, oval-shape fruit, known as sunflower seeds.

ENEMIES
The parasitic plant called the sunflower broomrape is the main threat to sunflower crops. It sucks energy from the plant, leaving the flower heads small.

COAST REDWOOD

The monumental giant of the forest

Reaching up to the clouds, these towering trees are the ultimate survivors—able to live for thousands of years, enduring wild winds, extreme temperatures, and even the flames of forest fires.

SCIENTIFIC NAME:
SEQUOIA SEMPERVIRENS

CLASS: Pinopsida
ORDER: Pinales
FAMILY: Cupressaceae

THE TREE GETS ITS NAME FROM THE BEAUTIFUL COLOR OF ITS BARK.

SUPER RESILIENCE

These enormous trees have adapted over millennia to survive nearly anything, including fire. Much of this resilience is due to the toughness of the tree's bark, which can grow to 1 foot thick and contains both water and a fire-resistant substance called tannin. This superpowered bark can even heal over scars that forest fires might leave.

SUPER REGENERATION

This irrepressible tree is able to sprout new growth from the bottom of its trunk after injury or fire damage. Even if a coast redwood falls, clone trees can shoot up from the stump or roots of the old tree, bringing new life to the forest.

SUPER LONGEVITY

The oldest-known specimen is an amazing 2,200 years old and foresters believe that there are older coast redwoods out there. The oldest trees are found in deep valleys and ravines with streams, where abundant fog provides them with the moisture they need to survive the long, dry summer months.

SUPER SEED

Coast redwoods produce small seeds in astonishing quantities—with a mature tree releasing about six million each year. However, it's not easy to germinate on the forest floor and only about 5 percent will develop into seedlings. Those lucky few are able to survive in the shady undergrowth of the forest for hundreds of years, waiting for just the right moment to begin their climb toward the sky.

SUPER TRUNK

The trunk of this tree can soar to unbelievable heights. A tree called Hyperion, in California's Redwood National Park, is the tallest living thing in the world, reaching the jaw-dropping height of 379 feet. And these giant trunks don't just grow upward, they also grow outward, with Hyperion measuring about 26 feet across at the bottom.

The canopy of the coast redwood forest is its own ecosystem and is home to many different species, including worms, lizards, and salamanders.

SIZE
The tallest trees on Earth, coast redwoods can grow to more than 375 feet tall.

COLOR
Reddish-brown bark, which darkens over time, and green leaves.

SPECIAL FEATURES
As coast redwoods grow, they lose their lower branches. This stops flames from reaching the canopy during forest fires.

LIFESPAN
Often at least 600 years but, in the right conditions, they can live for more than 1,000 years.

HABITAT
Native to the humid mountain ranges of the west coast of the United States, between southern Oregon and central California.

REPRODUCTION
Reproduces by seeds and stump sprouts.

ENEMIES
Other trees, such as oaks, pines, and firs, often invade the lands where the coast redwood grows. Climate change also threatens the delicate balance of the coast redwood forest ecosystem.

PASSION FRUIT

The colorful climber of the rain forest

This dramatic plant likes to make a statement. With showy flowers, evergreen leaves, and speedy vines that sprawl through the forest in search of sunlight, it's not one to hide in the shadows!

SCIENTIFIC NAME:
PASSIFLORA EDULIS

CLASS: Magnoliopsida
ORDER: Malpighiales
FAMILY: Passifloraceae

IN BRAZIL, THE PLANT WAS ORIGINALLY CALLED MARA KUYA, OR "FRUIT IN A BOWL."

SUPER MOBILITY

Always on the move, the vine of the passion fruit plant is able to climb up trees and rocks with impressive agility. Using coil-like shoots, called tendrils, to wind itself around nearby stems and branches, the vine makes its way higher and higher toward the canopy.

SUPER SPEED

If warmth, water, and sunshine are in abundance, this hasty plant can cover an area of more than 50 square feet in just a few short months.

SUPER FLOWER

With bright white petals and an explosion of purple filaments radiating out from the center, the flamboyant flower of the passion fruit plant has a theatrical appearance. But its striking looks aren't just for show—this complicated bloom is carefully designed to guide pollinators to the reproductive organs taking center stage in the middle.

SUPER FRUIT

Technically a berry, passion fruit has a thick rind to protect the precious seeds inside. It is highly nutritious and can be used in all kinds of food and beverages, from cake and ice cream to preserves, yogurt, and even tea.

SUPER SEED

Each passion fruit can contain between 180 and 200 seeds. This impressive haul increases the plant's chances of reproduction.

The plant's fruit is a good source of vitamins for both humans and animals. In some parts of the world, it is used in medicines for coughs, sleeplessness, and pain.

SIZE
The vines can grow to lengths of about 65 feet and, in the wild, the flowers can grow to around 2 inches across.

COLOR
White flowers with pink, red, or purple tinges. Dark green leaves on the vine.

SPECIAL FEATURES
The large, smooth leaves on the passion fruit vine are evergreen, keeping their color all year.

LIFESPAN
Normally no more than 10 years.

HABITAT
Native to the warm regions of Central and South America, this plant is now grown as a crop in tropical and subtropical regions around the world.

REPRODUCTION
Reproduces by seeds. Although the flowers have both male and female reproductive organs, they still rely on pollinators.

ENEMIES
It is the favorite food of the larvae of Juno silverspot butterflies, with caterpillars feeding on the buds, stems, and flowers of the plant.

TITAN ARUM

POWERS:

SCIENTIFIC NAME:
AMORPHOPHALLUS TITANUM

CLASS: Liliopsida
ORDER: Alismatales
FAMILY: Araceae

The stinking corpse flower

A celebrity of the plant world, titan arum's gigantic flowers are impressive masters of disguise. Their stomach-turning stench mimics that of rotting flesh, making them irresistible to both passing insects and plant lovers seeking out the quirkiest specimens on the planet.

OCCURRING ONLY THREE OR FOUR TIMES IN ITS 40-YEAR LIFESPAN, THIS PLANT'S FLOWERING IS UNMISSABLE.

SUPER
FLOWER
Known far and wide as the world's biggest flower, titan arum is actually an inflorescence, a type of flowering structure, but it's still absolutely massive. Made up of clusters of smaller flowers, all crowded together on a huge flower spike called a spadix, this gigantic structure can grow to a whopping 9 feet 9 inches tall.

SUPER
MIMICRY
This plant has another, much smellier, superpower—the flower has adapted to perfectly mimic the horrible stench of rotting flesh, attracting flies and other insects that like to eat dead animals. Tricked into believing they've found some decaying meat to feast on, the insects lay their eggs on the flower, pollinating it at the same time. Securing the title of the world's smelliest plant, titan arum's whiff has hints of garlic, rotting fish, and sweaty socks—yuck!

SUPER
SPEED
When it's time to bloom, this flower can shoot upward at a rapid speed of 4 inches a day until it reaches maturity. Using all that energy means the flower is famously fleeting, living for just two to three days. Thankfully, it only releases the disgusting smell for the first 12 to 24 hours.

SUPER
LONGEVITY
This plant can live for more than 40 years, but it might only flower three or four times during its long life. When not producing flowers, the plant sends up long stems with an umbrella of leaves at the top. These giant structures look like small trees, but they are, in fact, a single, gigantic leaf. They collect energy, which the plant stores, ready for the next big bloom. These periods without flowers, called latency, enable the plant to prolong its life.

The tip of the flower spike can heat up, wafting foul-smelling particles almost half a mile away from the plant, helping it to attract pollinators far and wide.

SIZE
Up to 9 feet 9 inches tall.

COLOR
The flower is green on the outside. It is a rich dark purple or red on the inside, another tactic to disguise itself as rotting flesh.

SPECIAL FEATURES
It has a clever underground storage organ called a root tuber, which stores food and water.

LIFESPAN
40 years.

HABITAT
Native to the tropical rain forests of Sumatra, Indonesia. The plant is now a main attraction at botanic gardens around the world, with its rare blooms drawing in thousands of visitors at a time.

REPRODUCTION
Reproduces by seeds. The yellow or red berries are popular with rhinoceros hornbills, which eat the fruit and disperse the seeds around the rain forest.

ENEMIES
This plant is almost extinct in the wild due to deforestation, overcollection, and other human activities.

JACKAL FOOD

SCIENTIFIC NAME:
HYDNORA AFRICANA

CLASS: Magnoliopsida
ORDER: Piperales
FAMILY: Hydnoraceae

The disappearing act

This secretive, leafless wonder has earned itself the title of "the strangest plant in the world." Lurking underground, it can be invisible for years at a time, but be sure that its bizarre flower and its sneaky survival strategies are well worth the wait.

THE PLANT IS KNOWN LOCALLY AS JAKKALSKOS, OR "JACKAL FOOD" IN THE AFRIKAANS LANGUAGE.

SUPER SUBSTANCES

The jackal food plant uses a clever mix of chemicals to give off a putrid smell, attracting beetles and other insects that feed on dead and decaying animals. Lured in by the pungent smell, they're trapped before they know it.

SUPER FLOWER

Every once in a while, after heavy rains, the jackal food plant sends a peach-colored flower up to the ground's surface. These curious flowers, made up of three fleshy petals, can trap insects, keeping them captive in a floral prison until they have pollinated the plant. The petals will then open, releasing the creature so that it can spread the pollen to other flowers. Once it has fruited, the plant disappears back underground.

SUPER INTELLIGENCE

Unlike most plants, the jackal food plant doesn't have leaves. This means that making its energy from sunshine, through photosynthesis, isn't an option. Instead, it has developed its own stealthy strategy. This plant is a parasite, meaning it steals water and nutrients from other plants, known as hosts, getting everything it needs to survive, without any of the hard work!

SUPER ROOTS

The jackal food plant chooses its victims carefully, selecting members of a family of flowering plants called *euphorbias*. The plant uses its thick, fleshy roots to attach to the roots of the host plant, sucking out the nutrients it needs.

SUPER RESILIENCE

Thriving in harsh conditions, this plant can grow in dry, poor-quality soil, go long stretches of time without water, and withstand extreme temperatures that would be too much for other plants to handle.

Baboons, jackals, porcupines, moles, and many kinds of birds eat the plant's fruit and disperse its seeds around the habitat.

SIZE
The flower can grow up to 1 foot across.

COLOR
Orangey red flowers and brown, gray, and black for the rest of the plant.

SPECIAL FEATURES
Similar in appearance to a fungus, this plant has no stem or leaves. It is made up of only roots and a flower.

HABITAT
Native to the semideserts of southern Africa. It is not found in the wild anywhere else in the world, because this is the only place where the host plants grow.

REPRODUCTION
Reproduces by seeds. Each fruit can contain up to 20,000 seeds.

ENEMIES
Destruction of its habitat and excessive harvesting for medicinal use have reduced this plant's numbers.

SKELETON FLOWER

The mysterious magician

If you hear the rumble of a rain cloud, grab your umbrella and get ready to witness something magical. This small white flower undergoes a spectacular transformation when it gets caught in the rain.

SCIENTIFIC NAME:
DIPHYLLEIA GRAYI

CLASS: Magnoliopsida
ORDER: Ranunculales
FAMILY: Berberidaceae

THIS PLANT'S SCIENTIFIC NAME, *DIPHYLLEIA*, MEANS "TWO LEAVES" IN GREEK.

SUPER
FLOWER

This plant might look ordinary at first glance, but wait until it rains and you'll see something truly magical happen. Right in front of your eyes, the normally white petals of the flower will become transparent, meaning you can see right through them! This show-stopping transformation is caused by the spongelike structure of the petals' cells, which changes how light rays reflect off its surface, depending on whether the plant is dry or wet. When wet, you can still see the veins inside the petals showing up like a floral skeleton, giving the plant its spooky name. As the rain passes and the petals dry out, the flowers return to their original white color. Scientists aren't exactly sure why the plant performs this trick, but it's beautiful to see!

SUPER
RESILIENCE

Although the skeleton flower's shimmering petals may be delicate, it's a surprisingly tough plant overall. It can survive in shady, damp places as well as those exposed to some sunlight. It can also manage with an impressively wide range of temperatures, from a frosty 45°F to a balmy 86°F.

Traditionally used to make natural dyes in parts of Asia, scientists are now investigating whether this plant may have medicinal properties that could help fight cancer.

SIZE
The plant can grow to 2 feet 3 inches tall and the flowers can grow to ¾ inch across.

COLOR
Green stems and leaves, and white or see-through flowers, depending on the weather. The fruit is a dark purplish-blue, growing on red stalks.

SPECIAL FEATURES
As if ready for the rain that will activate the magic trick, the plant has large, umbrella-shape leaves.

LIFESPAN
Dying down in winter and reappearing in spring, this plant can live for many years.

HABITAT
Native to moist, wooded mountainsides in the cooler regions of Japan, Russia, and the eastern United States.

REPRODUCTION
Reproduces by seeds. The plant's flowers have both male and female reproductive organs.

ENEMIES
Urban development is destroying the forests where this plant grows, threatening its survival.

STRANGLER FIG

The boa constrictor tree

SCIENTIFIC NAME:
FICUS AUREA

CLASS: Eudicotyledoneae
ORDER: Rosales
FAMILY: Moraceae

This parasitic tree steals nutrients, water, and even sunlight from its unsuspecting victims. Coiling itself around its host tree like a hungry snake, the strangler fig tightens its grip, killing and devouring its target.

KNOWN IN PERU AS "TREE KILLERS," THERE ARE MORE THAN 850 KINDS OF STRANGLER FIGS AROUND THE WORLD.

SUPER
INTELLIGENCE

This plant's seeds germinate high up in the canopy, in the branches of its chosen host tree. The plant's aerial roots absorb water and nutrients from their surroundings and the plant sends them downward, twisting around their host and constricting its growth. As the host begins to die, the fig digests nutrients released from the rotting wood. Eventually, the host tree will be no more and the strangler fig is left standing in its place. It's beautiful to see!

SUPER
TEAMWORK

Fig trees have what is known as a "mutualistic" relationship with particular kinds of wasps, meaning both the tree and the insect benefit from the bond. Each fig tree has its own species, or two at most, of "fig wasp." This specific wasp will be the only creature that can pollinate that specific tree and, in return, the tree provides the only suitable place for the wasp to lay their eggs.

SUPER
SUBSTANCES

When the female flowers reach maturity, they release a chemical substance that lures the female wasps in.

SUPER
MOBILITY

The seeds of this plant are often delivered to the treetops in the poop of birds, which will eat the fruit of one plant and then fly long distances before spreading the seeds. This expands the range of the species and also means that baby plants don't compete with parents for space, light, or food.

SUPER
FLOWER

The strangler fig carefully times its blooms to aid the plant's relationship with its wasp. Female flowers mature first, attracting female wasps, who lay their eggs and then die. Emerging young wasps, called larvae, eat some of the seeds and grow into adults. Just as the wasps are ready to mate, the female flowers die and the male flowers mature. The adult female wasps, now covered in pollen from the male flowers, head off in search of new female flowers so that they can lay their eggs, pollinating other figs along the way.

The strangler fig's fruit is an important food source for many birds and some animals, with its long fruiting season providing nutrients when other fruit is scarce.

SIZE
Up to 100 feet tall in the wild.

COLOR
Ash gray trunk, bright green leaves, and fruit that starts green and turns yellow when ripe.

SPECIAL FEATURES
It grows outward as well as down, with its branches stretching out to form a large and thick canopy.

LIFESPAN
This plant can live for many years.

HABITAT
Native to the tropical regions of Florida, as well as Mexico, certain countries in Central America, and across the Caribbean.

REPRODUCTION
Reproduces by seeds. Each tree produces both female and male flowers, pollinated with pollen from other trees.

SPOTTED SPIDER ORCHID

The tarantula trickster

SCIENTIFIC
NAME:
**BRASSIA
MACULATA**

CLASS: Liliopsida
ORDER: Asparagales
FAMILY: Orchidaceae

You'd probably do your best to avoid a huge, spider-eating wasp with one of the most painful stings on the planet, but the spotted spider orchid does just the opposite—using its lookalike flowers to lure in its chosen pollinator.

PRIZED FOR THEIR BEAUTY, ORCHIDS HAVE BEEN GROWN IN CHINA AND JAPAN FOR THOUSANDS OF YEARS.

SUPER
FLOWER

Sitting in a row along the plant's stem, with their slim, spotted petals, these long-lasting flowers are as pretty as a picture, and they even smell lovely, too. But dig a little deeper and you'll see that looks can be deceiving . . .

SUPER
ROOTS

Spotted spider orchids are usually epiphytes, meaning that they grow on the surface of other plants or trees, clinging on with their aerial roots. The orchids aren't parasitic, so they don't steal nutrients from these trees. Instead, they absorb food and water from the air around them, through a layer of special cells on their roots. This enables the plant to grow high up in the rain forest, where there is less competition for space, but they still have some shade from the scorching sun.

SUPER
MIMICRY

What may appear beautiful to us is, in fact, an elaborate disguise, aiming to lure in a particular, and terrifying, pollinator. The flower's petals imitate the long legs of a tarantula to attract a fierce insect called the tarantula hawk wasp. This wasp stings and paralyzes tarantulas, laying its eggs on the spider's bodies to provide food for its young when they hatch. Thinking the flower is a spider, the female wasps attack! Stinging and tugging at the flower again and again, they unknowingly collect pollen, which they then move to a new plant when they find another spider orchid and launch their next assault.

Orchids are one of the most ancient and adaptable plant families on Earth and they grow on every continent except Antarctica.

SIZE
The flowers can grow up to 8 inches long.

COLOR
Yellowish-green flowers with reddish-brown spots, and green leaves and stems.

SPECIAL FEATURES
It has podlike structures called pseudobulbs, which are used to store water.

LIFESPAN
This plant can live for many years, but ultimately it depends on the lifespan of the tree on which it grows.

HABITAT
Native to the dense tropical rain forests of Mexico, Central America, the West Indies, and the north of South America.

REPRODUCTION
Reproduces using dustlike seeds that are easily dispersed through the air.

DANDELION

The seeds that take to the skies

Flying over yards, parks, rivers, and sometimes even seas, the umbrella-like seeds of this familiar plant can cover impressive distances. So take a deep breath, blow as hard as you can, and don't forget to make a wish!

SCIENTIFIC NAME:
TARAXACUM OFFICINALE

CLASS: Magnoliopsida
ORDER: Asterales
FAMILY: Asteraceae

FOSSILIZED EARLY RELATIVES OF THE DANDELION DATE FROM ABOUT 50 MILLION YEARS AGO.

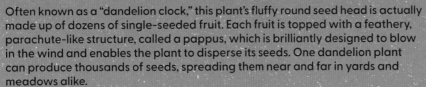

SUPER
SEED

Often known as a "dandelion clock," this plant's fluffy round seed head is actually made up of dozens of single-seeded fruit. Each fruit is topped with a feathery, parachute-like structure, called a pappus, which is brilliantly designed to blow in the wind and enables the plant to disperse its seeds. One dandelion plant can produce thousands of seeds, spreading them near and far in yards and meadows alike.

SUPER
MOBILITY

Each seed begins its journey when it is blown from the plant by the wind (or by people). While many of the seeds will land nearby, a small number will travel huge distances. In just the right conditions, they can soar through the skies for anywhere between 300 feet and 90 miles.

SUPER
FLOWER

The flower of a dandelion is actually a flower head made up of a mass of smaller flowers called ray florets. Although some gardeners think of dandelions as weeds, these golden-yellow flowers are rich in pollen and popular with pollinators.

SUPER
LEAF

The long leaves of this plant grow flat on the ground in a rosette shape. They have serrated, or jagged, edges that look like rows of spiky teeth. It's this distinctive shape that gave the plant its old French name, *dent de lion*, which means "lion's teeth." Roar!

The dandelion is an edible plant and its leaves can be used in salads.

SIZE
Between 2 and 15 inches tall.

COLOR
Green leaves and a yellow flower.

SPECIAL FEATURES
The stems remain leafless, with the leaves growing in a circle on the ground.

LIFESPAN
Normally five to ten years.

HABITAT
Widespread in the temperate regions of the world (areas characterized by mild temperatures, located between the tropics and the polar regions).

REPRODUCTION
Reproduces by seeds. Although they are visited by insects, most of the seeds are dispersed by the wind.

ENEMIES
Dandelions, although resilient, can be attacked by aphids, caterpillars, and whitefly.

SCIENTIFIC NAME:
CASTANEA SATIVA

CLASS: Magnoliopsida
ORDER: Fagales
FAMILY: Fagaceae

SWEET CHESTNUT

The sweet but spiky fruit tree

The elegant, towering trunk and golden flowers of this pretty tree may make it look like a gentle giant, but it has a spiky side and knows how to protect itself against hungry visitors.

THE TREE'S NAME COMES FROM THE GREEK VILLAGE OF KASTANAS, FAMOUS FOR ITS CHESTNUT WOODS.

SUPER
LONGEVITY

The oldest sweet chestnut trees usually grow in warm climates, with fertile, well-drained soil, plenty of sunlight, and protection from strong winds. In these conditions, a tree can live for between 200 and 500 years. The world's oldest-known sweet chestnut tree can be found growing on the side of the Mount Etna volcano in Sicily, Italy. This legendary tree is believed to be between 2,000 and 4,000 years old.

SUPER
TRUNK

Starting off smooth and green in younger trees, the trunk's bark will then turn from grayish-purple to brown, getting darker as the tree gets older. With time, the trunks develop vertical "fissures," or grooves, which eventually form a beautiful spiral, swirling up the tree toward its branches.

SUPER
PROTECTION

When the seeds are developing, they are covered with a superspiny case, called a burr, which acts as a kind of spiky armor, stopping any hungry creatures from breaking in and having a nibble.

SUPER
FLOWER

The sweet chestnut tree bursts into flower in the summertime, sending out long, fluffy flower spikes called catkins. These colorful blooms have a strong scent (which some people say smells like frying mushrooms) and are incredibly popular with pollinating insects, such as bees.

SUPER
 ## FRUIT

When the fruit is ripe, the case splits open and the edible nuts are released. Each nut has a velvety skin and a dark brown shell that is glossy and hard. The fruit gradually ripens between September and November, just in time for us to enjoy roasted chestnuts as a wintery treat!

The flowers provide nectar for bees and other pollinators and the delicious nuts are a source of food for birds, animals, and humans.

SIZE
Can grow up to 115 feet tall and spread to more than 40 feet wide. Its leaves can reach up to 1 foot long.

COLOR
Grayish-purple to brown bark and bright green leaves, turning golden in fall. Yellow flowers, green cases and red-brown fruit.

SPECIAL FEATURES
The tree's leaves have toothed edges and a pointed tip. Each leaf has about 20 pairs of prominent parallel veins.

LIFESPAN
Normally between 200 and 500 years.

HABITAT
Native to southern and southeastern Europe.

REPRODUCTION
Reproduces by seeds. Male and female flowers grow separately on the same tree.

ENEMIES
A deadly fungal infection called sweet chestnut blight devastated chestnut forests in the eastern United States during the first half of the 20th century, killing an estimated 3.5 billion trees.

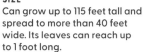

OLEANDER

The toxic terror

Also known as the rose laurel or rose bay, this striking plant packs a punch when it comes to poison. Warding off unwanted guests with a mix of toxins, it is definitely one to avoid if you're feeling hungry.

SCIENTIFIC NAME:

NERIUM OLEANDER

CLASS: Magnoliopsida
ORDER: Gentianales
FAMILY: Apocynaceae

IT IS SAID A WHOLE BATTALION OF NAPOLEAN'S ARMY WAS POISONED BY MEAT ROASTED ON OLEANDER BRANCHES.

SUPER
FLOWER

With its striking clusters of pink, yellow, white, or red flowers, this bright and beautiful plant is a celebration of color, blooming in spring and then again in late summer. But these pretty flowers are not the complete picture—in fact, they're hiding something much more sinister . . .

SUPER
SUBSTANCES

Behind its beautiful appearance, this plant is pretty toxic. Every part, from the roots and stems to the leaves and flowers, is poisonous. The plant's sap irritates the skin and inflames the eyes, while the rest can cause vomiting, stomachache, and an upset stomach if eaten. Large amounts can even lead to heart troubles. Its bitter and unpleasant taste are normally enough to put people off, but just to be safe, make sure to never eat fruit, flowers, or leaves if you don't know what they are and that they are safe to eat!

SUPER
RESILIENCE

This evergreen shrub can tolerate tough growing conditions, dealing with drought, heat, and the salty air typical of the Mediterranean regions where it originated.

SUPER
INTELLIGENCE

The plant's poisons are, in fact, a supersmart strategy to keep it safe, warding off threats, such as pests and grazing animals. In a clever twist, the strength of the poison in the plant's flowers is lower than elsewhere in the plant, meaning that welcome visitors, such as pollinating insects, are not harmed.

The oleander can build up a large concentration of pollutants, taking lead, zinc, and cadmium out of the soil around it, helping to keep its environment healthy.

SIZE
Up to 20 feet tall.

COLOR
Green leaves all year round and pink, yellow, white, or red flowers.

SPECIAL FEATURES
The young stems start out green but turn gray over time, and the spear-shape leaves are hard and thick.

LIFESPAN
Between 20 and 30 years.

HABITAT
Native to the Mediterranean. Today, it is found in most regions of the world that have a tropical or subtropical climate.

REPRODUCTION
Reproduces by seeds. The plant's small fruit contains seeds with a tiny parachute-like structure called a pappus, perfectly designed for air dispersal.

ENEMIES
Some insects, such as the oleander hawk moth (*Daphnis nerii*) and its caterpillars, are unaffected by the plant's poison so can feed on its leaves without worry.

POWERS:
✦ ✦
✦
✦ ✦

SENSITIVE PLANT

The perfect performer of the rain forest

A theatrical superstar, also called the shameplant, this odd little plant will close up its leaves if threatened. Pretending to wither and wilt, it escapes the hungry mouths of plant-eating insects and lives to fight another day.

SCIENTIFIC NAME:
MIMOSA PUDICA

CLASS: Magnoliopsida
ORDER: Fabales
FAMILY: Fabaceae

SCIENTISTS BELIEVE THE PLANT WILL REMEMBER IF A REPEATED DISTURBANCE IS NOT A THREAT AND STOP CLOSING ITS LEAVES.

SUPER SENSITIVITY

If touched, shaken, or even blown on, this hypersensitive plant will respond in a flash, folding up its compound leaves (made up of many, tiny leaflets), dropping down its leaf stem, and "hiding." This dramatic performance makes the plant look wilted, protecting it from plant-eating insects that prefer to nibble on fresh, green leaves instead of floppy, dying ones.

SUPER RESILIENCE

This plant grows easily in most types of soil and will quickly take advantage of any sunny space available. This impressive flexibility is thanks to its super roots, which can produce their own nitrogen instead of needing to collect it from the surrounding soil.

SUPER SPEED

The sensitive plant is one of the few plants in the world capable of "rapid movements," closing its leaves within seconds of contact. It uses a change in water pressure within the leaves' cells to achieve this speedy transformation.

SUPER INTELLIGENCE

This clever plant responds not just to touch, but also to temperature, light, and water. It will fold up overnight or during the hottest parts of the day to prevent water loss, as well as during bad weather to protect itself from rain and wind.

This plant has many medicinal benefits and is used for soothing cuts, treating an upset stomach, repairing damaged nerves, and healing snakebites.

SIZE
Up to about 1 foot 8 inches tall (this can stretch to 3 feet 3 inches when supported by other plants).

COLOR
Light green leaves and pale pink or pale purple flowers.

SPECIAL FEATURES
The plant has thorny branches as an extra layer of protection.

LIFESPAN
Normally about five years.

HABITAT
Native to the tropical rain forests of the Americas.

REPRODUCTION
Reproduces by seeds. It produces a large number of seedpods, each containing three to five seeds.

ENEMIES
This plant is vulnerable to attack by spider mites, especially when growing outside in the wild.

SANDBOX

The dynamite tree

Keep clear! This dangerous tree is not only poisonous and covered in supersharp spikes, but its exploding fruit shatters with such force that it can cause injury to anyone standing in its way.

SCIENTIFIC NAME:

HURA CREPITANS

CLASS: Magnoliopsida
ORDER: Malpighiales
FAMILY: Euphorbiaceae

THE TREE IS ALSO KNOWN AS THE "MONKEY NO-CLIMB," BECAUSE ITS SPINY TRUNK IS HARD TO SCALE.

SUPER FRUIT

The poisonous fruit of the sandbox tree looks like a miniature pumpkin. But unlike pumpkins, this fierce fruit is utterly explosive! After heavy rain, when the time is right and the fruit is ripe, listen out for a loud bang as it shatters, sending its seeds flying through the air with incredible force.

SUPER RESILIENCE

This sturdy tree grows in many different kinds of soil, including those with high levels of salt. It also tolerates prolonged drought and strong winds and is resistant to small wildfires.

SUPER PROTECTION

A champion of self-defense, this tree is loaded with clever strategies to ward off unwelcome visitors. Its highly toxic sap means that every part of the tree, from the bark to the leaves to the seeds, is poisonous. And just to add an extra layer of security, the tree's bark is covered with thousands of conical, pointed thorns—ouch!

SUPER SPEED

The soaring seeds are propelled from the tree at an amazing pace. They can reach speeds of 230 feet per second and cover distances of up to 150 feet, enabling the tree to colonize distant areas without having to compete with the surrounding plants for food, water, and sunlight.

This tree's huge leaves provide shade to the plants growing around it.

SIZE
Up to 165 feet tall, with a trunk up to 6 feet 8 inches wide and branches more than 65 feet long. The fruit measures about 2 to 3¼ inches across.

COLOR
Gray trunk with dark spines, green leaves, and greenish-yellow fruit and flowers.

SPECIAL FEATURES
Its heart-shape, leathery leaves can grow to 2 feet long.

LIFESPAN
It's a long-lived tree.

HABITAT
Native to the tropical regions of the Americas, particularly the Amazon rain forest and Orinoco River Basin. It has been introduced to Australia and parts of Central Africa, and is an invasive plant in Tanzania, Kenya, and Uganda.

REPRODUCTION
Reproduces by seeds. Each tree produces both female and male flowers. The seeds can float, so they can also be dispersed by floods.

ENEMIES
This seemingly invincible tree has no significant enemies.

POWERS:

WHISTLING THORN

SCIENTIFIC
NAME:

VACHELLIA DREPANOLOBIUM

CLASS: Magnoliopsida
ORDER: Fabales
FAMILY: Fabaceae

The musical tree of the savanna

From pointy spikes and clever chemicals to roping in colonies of vicious ants to fight its corner, this hero of self-defense does all that it can to fend off hungry attackers.

ITS NAME COMES FROM THE EERIE SOUND CREATED AS WIND PASSES THROUGH HOLES MADE BY ANTS IN ITS THORNS.

SUPER
PROTECTION

This formidable tree has thin, spiky thorns that defend its leaves and branches against animals looking to feed on them. The leaves can also release bitter-tasting tannins, which make them tough and difficult to digest. While some large plant eaters try to munch their way through regardless, others are put off, opting for a tastier, less-spiky snack.

Despite the tree's best efforts, its leaves and small branches are an important food source for the herbivores of the savanna, particularly black rhinoceros and giraffes.

SUPER
TEAMWORK

This tree has a mutualistic relationship with a specific species of ant—this is a bond from which they both benefit. Some of the tree's thorns grow from bulbous nodes, and colonies of ants use these as their homes, feeding on the nectar produced by the tree. In return, the ants fiercely defend the trees against hungry herbivores. If an animal, such as an elephant, comes to graze on the tree, the ants will aggressively attack the predator. It's a win-win situation for both tree and ant, but not for the elephant!

SUPER
RESILIENCE

This tough and rugged tree survives the frequent wildfires that affect the regions where it grows.

SUPER
SUBSTANCES

Using a mix of chemical substances, these remarkable trees have developed the superspecial skill of communication. In places with multiple whistling thorns, if one tree is attacked, it will respond by releasing a kind of scent signal into the air, alerting other trees in the area to the threat. Following the warning, the trees immediately secrete a toxic substance into their leaves, which can be harmful to touch and eat, therefore putting off the predator and keeping the community of trees safe.

SIZE
Up to 20 feet tall.

COLOR
Grayish bark, green leaves, and pale yellow flowers.

SPECIAL FEATURES
This tree is nitrogen-fixing, meaning it can convert nitrogen in the air into useful nitrogen compounds in the soil, increasing the soil's fertility.

LIFESPAN
Normally up to 30 years.

HABITAT
Native to the East African savanna.

REPRODUCTION
Reproduces by seeds. The seeds are contained in a seedpod, measuring 4 to 8 inches in length.

ENEMIES
The tree's main threats are overgrazing from large herbivores and tree clearance for farming and urban development.

POWERS:

QUAKING ASPEN

The trembling giant of giants

THE QUAKING ASPEN GETS ITS NAME FROM ITS FLUTTERING LEAVES THAT QUIVER IN EVEN THE SLIGHTEST BREEZE.

SCIENTIFIC NAME:
POPULUS TREMULOIDES

CLASS: Magnoliopsida
ORDER: Malpighiales
FAMILY: Salicaceae

It's hard to believe, but if you were to look out over a huge forest of quaking aspens, with millions of leaves fluttering in the wind in front of your eyes, you could actually be looking at a single living thing. Get ready to meet the world's largest tree!

SUPER
TEAMWORK

While the stems of the quaking aspen look to us like individual trees, they are, in fact, all stems of one humungous organism. Each one has identical genes, and they are connected underground by an immense root system, creating a giant grove or a "colony of clones." In Fishlake National Forest in the Utah, you can find 47,000 quaking aspens in a single colony that covers about 105 acres. It has been given the name Pando, which means "I spread" in Latin, and it is the largest living thing on our planet—now that's teamwork!

SUPER
REGENERATION

Quaking aspens have an unusual way of reproducing. New specimens are born when the root of a parent tree expands and sends fresh stems up to the surface, in a process called suckering.

SUPER
ROOTS

The clever roots of the quaking aspen help the tree survive wildfires. Sitting safely underground, the roots are protected from the deadly flames above. When the fire is over, the roots swiftly send up new shoots and begin to grow afresh.

SUPER
LONGEVITY

The oldest stems in a colony die off naturally, but they are continually replaced by new clones, so this incredible organism can live for what seems like forever. It is difficult to say exactly how old Pando is and scientists have differing opinions, but even the lower estimates put it at the grand old age of 8,000 to 12,000 years.

SUPER
MOBILITY

Quaking aspen clone colonies are able to send new stems up to the ground as far as 50 miles away from the parent tree, meaning they can cover huge areas. The tree's tiny seeds are also built to travel, being covered in fluffy hairs that aid wind dispersal.

The leaves of the quaking aspen provide food for butterfly and moth caterpillars.

SIZE
Up to 115 feet tall.

COLOR
Grayish-green bark and green leaves that have a whitish underside.

SPECIAL FEATURES
The rounded leaves have toothed edges and a long, flat leaf stalk that causes them to flutter.

LIFESPAN
Individual stems can live for up to 150 years, but a clone colony as a whole can live for tens of thousands of years.

HABITAT
Native to cooler areas of North America.

REPRODUCTION
Reproduces by seeds and, more commonly, by cloning.

ENEMIES
Overgrazing by cattle and wild animals, such as deer and elk. Grazing prevents new suckers from growing and replacing stems as they die.

WELWITSCHIA

POWERS:
★★★
★★
★

The living fossil

This unique and ancient species has been growing, almost unchanged, for thousands of years. It is a true survivor, giving us clues of what the world may have been like in times gone by.

SCIENTIFIC NAME:
WELWITSCHIA MIRABILIS

CLASS: Gnetopsida
ORDER: Welwitschiales
FAMILY: Welwitschiaceae

AN ICON OF THE NAMIB DESERT, THIS PLANT APPEARS ON NAMIBIA'S NATIONAL COAT OF ARMS.

SUPER
LONGEVITY

Perfectly adapted for life in their arid desert homes, some individual specimens are thought be more than 2,000 years old.

SUPER
LEAF

This strange plant has just two leaves. It keeps them for the entirety of its existence, and they grow along the ground at a constant rate of about 3¼ to 6 inches a year. They do this continuously, sometimes for thousands of years at a time. The leaves can become shredded and their tips deteriorate as they are blown around on the sand, but they can still reach up to 20 feet long.

SUPER
INTELLIGENCE

Living deep in the Namib desert, where temperatures soar and there is hardly any rain at all, the welwitschia has developed a clever coping strategy to collect water. The leaves have a large number of stomata, or tiny openings, on their surface, enabling them to capture water from fog and dew. Their special shape then works as a funnel, directing the water down to the plant's roots.

SUPER
ROOTS

They have a central root, called a taproot, which reaches about 30 feet long. A network of fine roots then grows out from it into the stony soil, reaching impressive depths of up to 100 feet underground.

SUPER
TEAMWORK

This plant has built a strong relationship with a small insect known as the welwitschia bug (*Probergrothius angolensis*). The tiny creature is essential for pollinating the plant and, in return, it feeds on the welwitschia's sap.

SUPER
RESILIENCE

This tough plant has adapted perfectly to survive in soaring temperatures, nutrient-poor soil, and with little water—what a trooper!

Desert animals, such as zebras, oryx, and black rhinoceros, feed on the leaves of welwitschia. It provides a vital source of water in their hot, dry habitat.

SIZE
Up to about 3 feet 3 inches tall, with its leaves reaching up to 20 feet long.

COLOR
Green leaves.

SPECIAL FEATURES
The plant has a central, woody trunk that can store water.

LIFESPAN
Normally about 500 to 600 years, but some of the oldest plants are thought to be 2,000 years old.

HABITAT
Native to Namibia and Angola on the southwestern coast of Africa.

REPRODUCTION
Reproduces by seeds. The seeds have "wings," about ¾ inch long, that help them to be dispersed in the wind. They produce up to 10,000 seeds but only a few of these germinate.

ENEMIES
Climate change threatens the welwitschia plant, because desert environments are becoming increasingly dry and difficult to live in.

★ ★
★ ★

ROOTLESS DUCKWEED

The small but mighty multiplier

SCIENTIFIC NAME:
WOLFFIA ARRHIZA

CLASS: Liliopsida
ORDER: Alismatales
FAMILY: Araceae

At home in freshwater ponds with still or slow-moving water, this tiny aquatic plant is one of the smallest flowering plants on Earth. But watch out, it's quick to multiply and can soon form dense mats over the water's surface.

SUPER MOBILITY

Most plants are anchored in some way, often rooted in the soil or clinging onto rocks or other plants. But this wild card lives by its own rules. It has no true roots and lives untethered, floating freely on the surface of the water.

SUPER TEAMWORK

This tiny plant prefers to be part of a team! It grows in huge colonies, with thousands of individual plants grouping together to form thick green carpets over the water's surface.

SUPER SPEED

Duckweed can reproduce incredibly quickly, with the youngest plants growing fast and reaching reproductive maturity in an especially short time. If the conditions are right, its population can double in as little as four days.

SUPER INTELLIGENCE

Although this plant may look incredibly simple (it has no stem, no roots, and only a few tiny leaves), its internal structure is surprisingly complex. It is cleverly designed to float on the water, meaning it can obtain the sunlight it needs for photosynthesis while also absorbing the minerals and nutrients that it needs. When exposed to the cold, this resourceful plant becomes dormant, sinking down and waiting for warmer weather to return.

In certain countries in Southeast Asia, including Laos, Thailand, and Myanmar, rootless duckweed is considered a superfood, because it is so high in protein.

SIZE
Measures between $\frac{1}{32}$ and $\frac{3}{64}$ inch in length and weighs about $\frac{1}{64}$ ounce.

COLOR
Dark green.

SPECIAL FEATURES
It produces a fruit so small that it is invisible to the naked eye.

LIFESPAN
Each individual plant has a short life cycle of less than one month.

HABITAT
Native to Malaysia and Australia. It has spread throughout warm and sunny regions all over the world.

REPRODUCTION
Reproduces both by seeds and, more frequently, by cloning.

ENEMIES
Destruction of its natural habitat is making it difficult for rootless duckweed to grow in the wild.

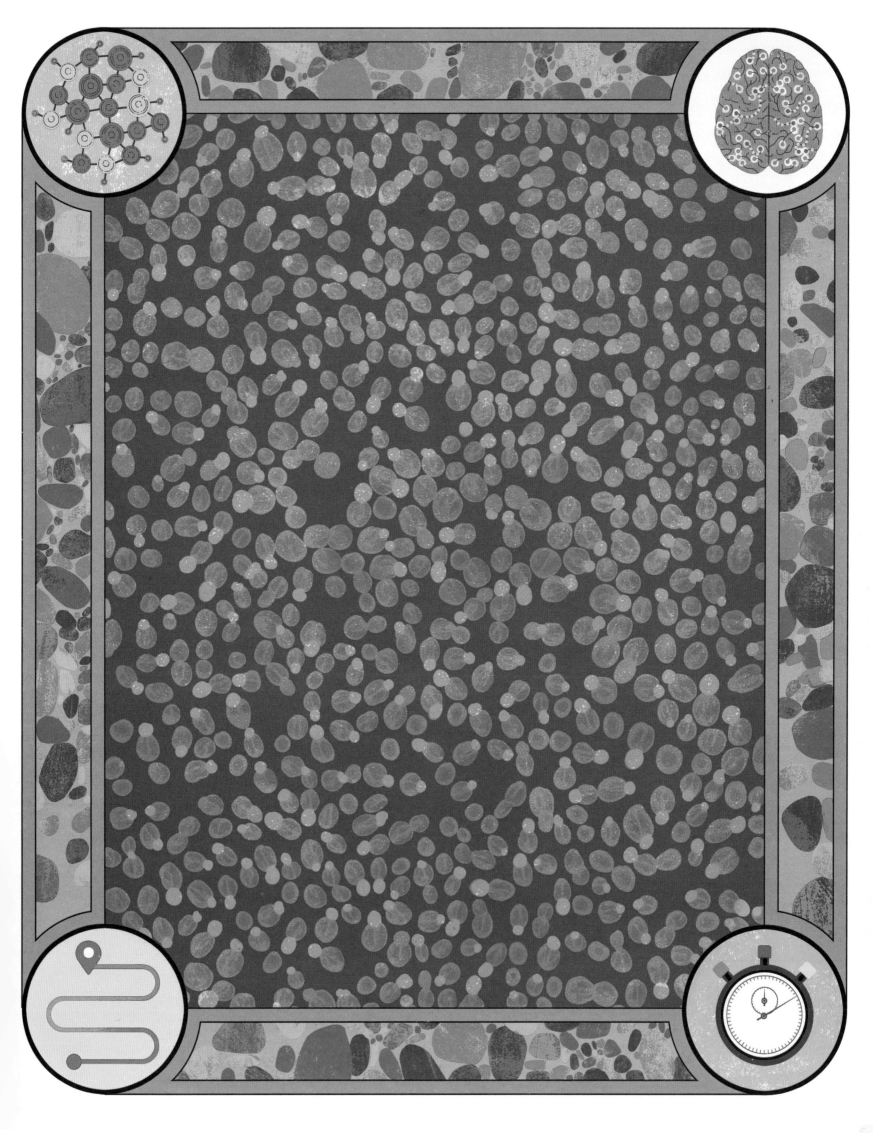

Phaidon Press Inc.
111 Broadway
New York, NY 10006

phaidon.com

This edition © 2025 Phaidon Press Limited
First published as *Superpoders de les plantes* by Zahorí Books
Sicília, 358 1-A · 08025 Barcelona
www.zahoribooks.com

Text © Soledad Romero Mariño 2024
Illustrations © Sonia Pulido 2024

ISBN 978 1 83866 951 5 (US edition)

006-0125

A CIP catalog record for this book is available from the Library of Congress.

Printed in China

Scientific Editing: Matilde Barón (CSIC)
Design and Layout: Joana Casals
Editing: Mar Valls

Edited by: Maya Gartner
Production by: Rebecca Price
Translated by: Cillero & de Motta

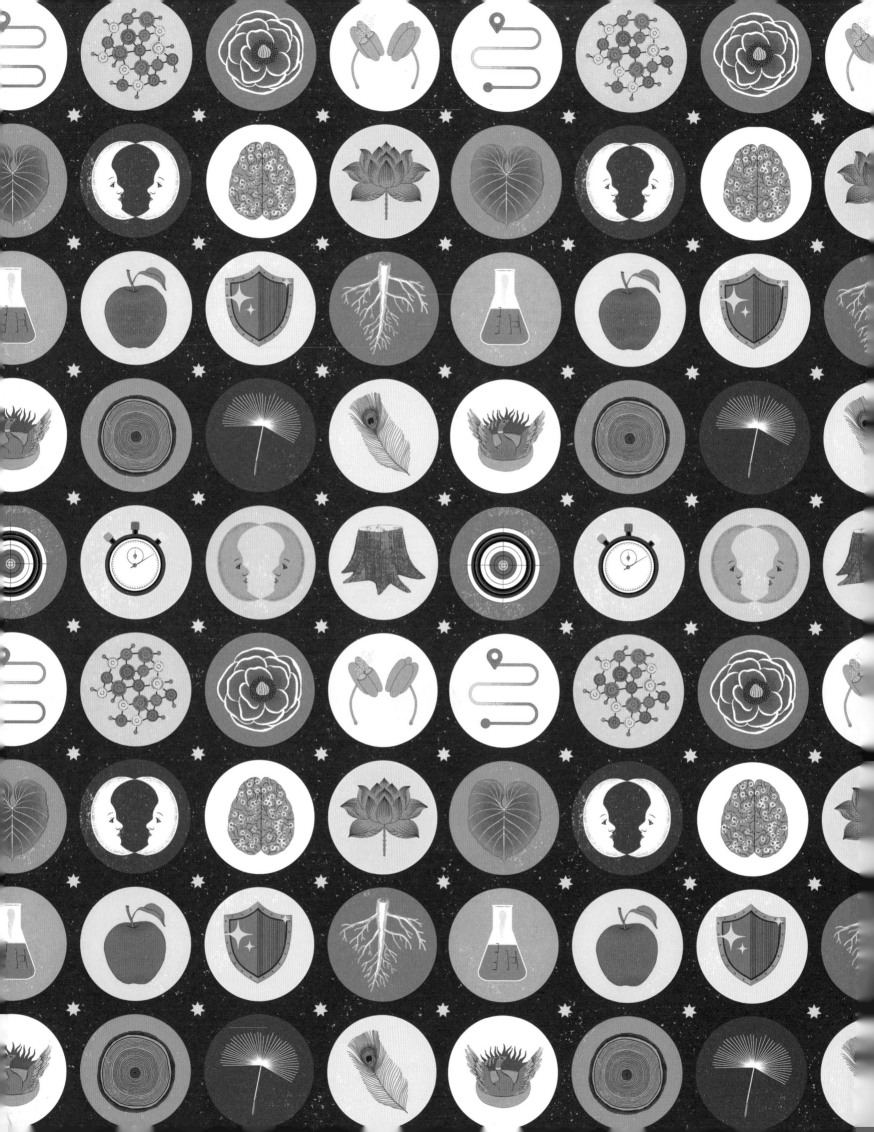